Down My Street

Written by Narinder Dhami

Illustrated by Nez Riaz

Collins

"Today we are starting an important and interesting topic," said Miss Blair. "It will be on the street you come from."

"But my street is not interesting, Miss!" Brook groaned.

When the lessons ended, Brook left for Green Street. His street had a corner shop, a hairdresser's and blocks of flats.

Brook's dad was gossiping with Dwight Foster from the flat upstairs.

"I have to do a topic on Green Street," Brook complained with a scowl. "But it's *so* boring!"

"No, Green Street is splendid!"
Dwight exclaimed.

"When I was a toddler, I remember travelling here with my mum," Dwight explained.

"I felt a little frightened. We ended up in Green Street. It was hard, but we liked the street."

Then Jasminder approached on her scooter.

"Brook!" Jasminder greeted him. "Look, my elder sister cooked pakoras today."

"Thanks, Jas!" Brook exclaimed.

Jasminder scooted off. Just then, Steena jogged out of her flat.

"I'm training for a marathon, Brook,"
Steena explained.

"A marathon?" said Brook.
"Fantastic!"

"Marc thinks Green Street is perfect," said Dad.

"We agree!" exclaimed Akbar, Yelda and Amjad.

"We fled Damascus when there was fighting," Akbar explained. "We were frightened. It was a long, hard trip."

"And we have remained in Green Street for years," Yelda added.

Then Brook understood. "Green Street is not interesting, but *we* are!" he exclaimed. "Now I can do my topic for Miss Blair!"

Brook's topic on Green Street

Green Street

Snips Hairdresser's

My block of flats

Brown's Corner Shop

My block of flats

Steena

1254

Akbar, Yelda and Amjad

Jasminder, her mum and dad and her sisters

Dwight Foster

Dad, Marc and me

Dwight likes cooking.

Marc loves to go
to sporting events.

Steena is training for
a marathon.

Yelda paints portraits.

Jasminder loves maths.

Brook's feelings

Review: After reading

Use your assessment from hearing the children read to choose any GPCs, words or tricky words that need additional practice.

Read 1: Decoding

- Encourage the children to read these words. Point out how "-ed" is often read as just "d": **complained exclaimed pakoras approached frightened**
- Challenge the children to take turns to read a page fluently aloud, and without pausing to sound out and blend. Say: Can you blend the words in your head when you read your page?

Read 2: Prosody

- Ask the children to work in groups of three to read the dialogue on pages 14 and 15. Each child in the group reads one of the character's words.
- Ask the children to think about how each character is feeling, for example, ask: How might Akbar feel when he remembers the fighting? Ask: Why is the word **we** in Brook's speech in italics? (e.g. *because Brook is excited*)
- After some preparation time, encourage the groups to read their parts to the group for positive feedback.

Read 3: Comprehension

- Ask the children to describe the street or area where they live. Do they like living there? Why?
- Read page 2 and then page 15. Ask: What has Brook discovered? (*that the people are exciting, which means the street isn't boring*)
- On page 7, discuss the meaning of the words **ended up** and **hard**.
  - o Ask the children to read pages 6 and 7, and explain what **ended up** means (e.g. *got to, settled in*). Discuss how the phrase suggests that they stayed in Green Street by chance.
  - o Point to **hard** on page 7. Ask: What does Dwight mean by **hard**? (e.g. *difficult*) Encourage the children to think about why life might have been hard for Dwight. (e.g. *he was a "toddler", "frightened" and he was far from his home*)
- Ask the children to take turns to hot-seat Brook and describe how Brook feels about the people in Green Street. They can use pages 22 and 23 to remind them of the characters. Ask: How do you feel about Jas, and why? (e.g. *I like her because she is kind to bring me pakoras*); What do you think of Steena? Why? (e.g. *I'm impressed because a marathon is a big challenge*); What do you think of Akbar and Yelda after hearing their story? (e.g. *I think they are brave*)
- Bonus content: Look together at pages 16 and 17, and think up new characters who live or work in Green Street. Ask: What makes each of the characters interesting? Ask: What pictures and captions could you imagine adding to pages 20 and 21?